INGRID BE

A Life from Beginning to End

Copyright © 2021 by Hourly History.

Table of Contents

Introduction

Celebrated actress Ingrid Bergman was born in Stockholm, Sweden, on August 29, 1915. She was much loved by her parents and had an almost idyllic early childhood until her mother died when she was barely three years old. This tragedy was followed by the death of her father eleven years later, leaving Bergman orphaned at age fourteen.

Her dream had always been to become an actress, and a few years after her father's passing, she was admitted into the prestigious Royal Dramatic Theatre School in Stockholm. Soon, Ingrid came to the attention of producer David O. Selznick and was offered a contract in America, which she accepted. There, she was an immediate success and had a long list of popular movies to her credit, such as *Intermezzo*, *Casablanca*, *For Whom the Bell Tolls*, and many others. The movies in which she starred have since become a part of Hollywood legend.

In Sweden, Bergman was married to Petter Lindström, a neurosurgeon. With her success in Hollywood, she moved her husband and their daughter Pia to Los Angeles. As their marriage became more strained, Ingrid met Italian director

Roberto Rossellini, and their affair and subsequent marriage scandalized America and the rest of the world. Bergman was ostracized from Hollywood and spent the next several years making movies in Europe. When she and Rossellini divorced, she slowly returned to make films in Hollywood. The divorce cost her considerable time with their two daughters because Rossellini refused to let them come to America. It would be many years until Ingrid eventually reconciled with her girls.

Ingrid Bergman made many sacrifices to enjoy both love and a career. She was among the first generation of women who felt that a woman, even an actress, should be able to have both. At the end of her long career, she had won three Oscars, two Emmys, one Tony, and four Golden Globe Awards—not an insignificant legacy for a woman who was denounced by Congress for her scandalous private life.

Chapter One

Ingrid, the Orphan

*"I have grown up alone. I've taken care of myself.
I worked, earned money and was independent at
18."*

—Ingrid Bergman

Anyone who believes that *Casablanca* is the ultimate romantic movie would probably enjoy the story of Ingrid's parents. Her parents exuded more than enough romance for Hollywood films.

Justus Bergman was a Swedish painter with a restless itch to travel. He wandered throughout Europe and even visited America, eking out a very meager living as a painter. He could not have been happier with his free-spirited lifestyle. During a stay in Kiel, Germany, he encountered Friedel, a girl still in her teens and 13 years younger than him. Friedel kept returning day after day to watch Justus paint. Soon, the two fell in love and were eager to get married. Friedel's parents immediately put an end to this little fling. They wanted more for their lovely young daughter. This older man, without a penny in the bank and absolutely no future, did not fit their image of a husband. And he was a foreigner to boot. No such man was worthy of their precious little girl.

But this foreigner did not give up. Justus abandoned his painting and turned it into a mere weekend hobby. He then opened a photography business that turned into quite a success. For many years, the couple was apart but remained hopeful and faithful. Justus saved every penny he could. After seven long years, he approached Friedel's father and simply handed him his bankbook, which now contained a considerable amount of money. Although Justus still wasn't their dream son-in-law, Friedel's parents were impressed. Reluctantly, they gave their consent to the marriage, and Justus and Friedel were married in 1907.

The couple went to create a home in Justus' native Sweden, where they were deliriously happy. To add to their incredible joy, their daughter Ingrid was born in the summer of 1915. Could their life get any better? Justus began to take hundreds and thousands of photographs of his little daughter. Ingrid herself later said she learned to pose for movies by posing for her father.

When Ingrid was about two and a half years old, the joy brutally ended when Friedel became ill and died. Ingrid never remembered much of her mother—she was too young—but she still had her adored father. She later said that "I had a wonderful childhood. I believed that my life with my father was perfect."

Each summer, Justus took Ingrid to Germany to visit her German grandparents and her mother's sisters. They were good people but much stricter than the free-spirited Justus. Still, Ingrid enjoyed her visits, especially to her aunt Elsa. Elsa had married rich and loved to shop for expensive things. When Ingrid stayed with her, Elsa inundated her with sophisticated clothes and other goodies. These were far too sophisticated for any preteen, but Ingrid loved it. What girl wouldn't?

When she was nine years old, her father hired a young woman named Greta as her nanny. Ingrid adored Greta. Since she could barely remember her mother, she felt no guilt about those feelings. Nor did she mind in the least when Justus became friendly with Greta and was showing signs of turning the relationship into something more permanent. Her German relatives, however, once again disapproved of Justus' ways. They bad-mouthed Greta at every opportunity until she moved out of the house. Ingrid missed her a great deal. Years later, she found out that Justus had wanted to marry Greta, but family opposition had stopped him.

Ingrid was 13 years old when her father's health deteriorated. Sadly, he soon died of stomach cancer in 1929. Since all she ever had was her father, the loss was devastating to Ingrid. Over the next few years, she lived with her various aunts and uncles. Her life changed from a daily joyous existence to a daily routine. Her relatives were practical people with none of the *joie de vivre* Ingrid had known with her father.

One day, by sheer coincidence, Ingrid ran into her old friend and nanny, Greta. Greta was working as an extra in the Swedish film industry. She appeared in crowd scenes which most movies have in abundance. Intrigued, Ingrid asked Greta if she could get her some work on set. On her first day as an extra, Ingrid left the studio with ten Swedish crowns in her pocket. It was the first money she had earned as an actress. She now was certain what she would do with her future.

At this time, Ingrid spent most of her time with her uncle Otto and aunt Hulda. They were good people and wanted the best for Ingrid, and they did not consider acting in Ingrid's best interest. As far as they were concerned, actresses were "tainted" women with a questionable reputation. That wouldn't do for their niece. Women were by now becoming more independent and were taking jobs such as secretaries or sales clerks. This was the path they wanted for Ingrid—safe, predictable, and respectable.

Ingrid continued to plead her case for enrolling in the Royal Dramatic Theatre School. Finally, her uncle Otto made a deal with her. He would let her try out for enrollment and allow her to attend if she won a coveted seat. She would only get one try. Since most of the students who auditioned didn't make it, Otto felt it was a fairly safe agreement. After getting this acting notion out of her system, Ingrid would settle down as a proper secretary, or so he thought.

Chapter Two

Becoming an Actress

"If you took acting away from me, I'd stop breathing."

—Ingrid Bergman

Passing the entrance examination for the Royal Dramatic Theatre School was critical to Ingrid. She had only one dream; if she couldn't turn that dream into reality, what was left for her? She did not share her family's vision of working a desk job.

The exam required each applicant to perform two skits which would be judged by a panel. The successful ones would receive their good news in a white envelope. The rest could expect a brown envelope filled with different career suggestions. Most aspiring actors did dramatic scenes to showcase their dramatic ability, but Ingrid hoped she would stand out by doing comedy.

While she was performing her first skit, the judges didn't seem to pay attention to her.

Instead, they were talking amongst themselves. When she was done, they asked her to leave the stage without doing the required second scene. Filled with despair, Ingrid bolted from the building. She spent the rest of the day wandering the streets of Stockholm in tears. It felt like her life had just been ripped from her. She had promised her uncle she wouldn't try for a second admission, and realizing how supportive her father would have been only made the rejection more depressing. By her own admission, she considered suicide.

When Ingrid finally reached home, her cousin told her that a fellow actor friend who had also been at the audition had called. When Ingrid called him back, he told her that he had received his white winner's envelope and asked her why she hadn't grabbed her envelope. Didn't she know what it meant? Morosely, Ingrid told him she indeed knew what the color meant. Did he even know what the color of her envelope was? He definitely knew and told her. Ingrid slammed down the phone and raced back to the school to her envelope, which she had ignored on her way out. It was white. By some miracle, she had been admitted to the Royal Dramatic Theatre School.

The excitement flowing through her was unimaginable.

Years later, Ingrid encountered one of the judges and asked why she had been told to leave before doing her second scene. He said that she had been so confident in her first scene, the panel didn't want to waste valuable audition time by having her continue to perform when they already knew she was being admitted.

Ingrid loved her time at the school, where she was learning actual acting techniques for the first time. She was shy off-stage, though. Now at the age of 18, she still didn't have a boyfriend. Her cousin decided to set up a double date between her and a friend in an attempt at matchmaking. Ingrid found her blind date, Petter Lindström, quite attractive. He was an older man who paid for everyone's meal and even had a car. At this time, he was a dentist, but he had plans to continue his studies and practice as a surgeon.

Ingrid could barely get any words out and spent most of the date silently blushing. She was stunned when he asked if he might call her for another date. She immediately said yes. It was the beginning of many more dates, during which Ingrid fell in love. She soon couldn't abide a single day without seeing him. Since he spent every day tending to his patients, she wandered mindlessly through the days until she could see him in the evening.

A friend of Ingrid's uncle knew the director of Svensk Filmindustri, Gustaf Molander, and arranged for a movie audition. When Ingrid saw the result of her screen test, all she could see were flaws. Molander, however, saw a wealth of talent and potential. She received a role in the 1935 film *The Count of Monk's Bridge,* which led to other movie roles. Soon, Ingrid Bergman was working as much as she wanted as she earned herself a name in the Swedish film industry.

In March of 1936, her uncle Otto died. Petter remained at her side, and Ingrid brought him to her German relatives in Hamburg. They were now engaged, and she wanted that side of her family to approve her choice of husband. Petter, with his respectable profession as a physician, did make a good impression, and they were married on March 1, 1937.

The following year, Ingrid went to Berlin's UFA studios to star in a German film called *The Four Companions.* Thanks to her summers spent in Germany as a child, she spoke fluent German and had no trouble stepping into the role of Marianne Kruge. The country itself had, however, drastically changed since those carefree days. Hitler was now a visible presence everywhere, and the entire nation seemed engulfed in turmoil and fear. The director of the film took Ingrid to a Hitler rally, where everyone raised their right arm and shouted "*Heil*!" The director told her it was best not to call attention to herself and follow everyone else. Ingrid refused. She sat silently, feeling very uncomfortable; this was not her grandparents' Germany.

The infamous Nazi Minister of Propaganda Joseph Goebbels had already noticed the young Swedish actress. Ingrid learned that this could mean a multi-movie contract at a far higher salary than she could ever dream about in Sweden. She was told that, of course, Goebbels would expect certain favors in return. Ingrid became extremely nervous. Luckily, when first Goebbels saw her in person, he lost interest. "She's too tall!" snapped the 5-foot-5 Hitler aide.

Ingrid had hoped for three more German films, but she did not make another movie in Germany. She would not return to the country until the Second World War was over. Instead, she rushed home to Sweden as quickly as she could. At the end of the year, on September 20, 1938, Petter and Ingrid's daughter, Pia, was born.

Around this time, Ingrid was approached by American movie mogul David O. Selznick to do a remake of her Swedish film *Intermezzo*. Selznick's representative had specifically traveled to Sweden to convince her to redo her original character for an American version with Leslie Howard. Her contract was for $2,500 a week, and it was a seven-year contract. This was tremendous news. It also called for a risky decision. What if Ingrid failed in America? Still, she was willing to try. Leaving Petter and Pia in Sweden, she sailed to the United States in 1939. She assumed she would be back as soon as filming for *Intermezzo* had wrapped up.

Chapter Three

Leaving Sweden Behind

"I have no regrets. I wouldn't have lived my life the way I did if I was going to worry about what people were going to say."

—Ingrid Bergman

Ingrid took the *Queen Mary* to New York in the spring of 1939, spending two weeks in New York before taking the train to California. She loved the Big Apple, with its museums, tall buildings, and Broadway plays. She was also delighted by banana splits. Ingrid would always have a sweet tooth.

When she finally met David O. Selznick, it turned out he had some concerns about his new protégé. Ingrid was too tall (5 foot 9, or 175 centimeters), she did not speak English very well, and her name sounded German, not a good thing as the war against Nazi Germany was intensifying. Also, in the era of Joan Crawford-style plucked eyebrows, her eyebrows were too thick.

It turned out that her co-star, Leslie Howard, was slightly taller than Ingrid, so that didn't turn into an issue. However, since she was already known as Ingrid Bergman in Europe, she refused to change her name, nor did she want to pluck her eyebrows. Luckily, Ingrid was so incredibly beautiful, few men argued with her, and that included David O. Selznick. Her English improved fast enough for her to do the film, and while she always criticized her own accent, Americans found it charming.

Her first American movie, *Intermezzo*, was a story about adultery. In *Intermezzo*, Leslie Howard plays Holger Brandt, a well-known violinist, who meets his daughter's piano teacher, Anita Hoffman, played by Ingrid. He offers to bring her along on his next tour. As Holger and Anita continue touring, they fall in love, and Holger's wife kicks him out.

Anita feels overwhelming guilt at keeping Holger from the son and daughter he loves so much. She cannot bear breaking up a family and leaves to tour on her own. Holger goes home and visits his daughter, Ann Marie, at her school. To his horror, as she runs toward him, she is hit by a passing car. Holger is relieved when he finds out that his daughter will survive her injuries. He returns home to his forgiving family.

Selznick had barely made any changes from the Swedish version, which had won high praises in Sweden, and felt very strongly about doing a close imitation of the original. Director William Wyler absolutely disagreed. They argued, but Selznick refused to give in, and Wyler was fired. Already, the heretofore unknown Swedish actress was causing a stir. While Leslie was unable to play the violin well enough for closeups, Ingrid had been playing the piano all her life, and they were able to shoot her own fingers playing complicated melodies.

Intermezzo is a simple morality tale that introduced Ingrid Bergman to her new American audience. Selznick could not have chosen a better movie. Her fresh, glowing radiance is stunning. Everyone in Hollywood knew that a new star had just been born. Everyone, that is, except Ingrid Bergman. She finished the picture and returned home to Sweden, missing the triumphant premiere of *Intermezzo*. Instead, she shot another Swedish movie. She was barely done when Selznick's office was on the phone to remind her of the seven-year contract that was still open. Ingrid soon returned to America with her daughter Pia. Petter, who had joined the army, could not come with them immediately. They would have to spend some time apart.

Chapter Four

Casablanca

"There are only seven movie stars in the world whose name alone will induce American bankers to lend money for movie productions, and the only woman on the list is Ingrid Bergman."

—Cary Grant

When Ingrid returned to the United States, she very much hoped to be cast in a project about Joan of Arc. Unfortunately, Selznick wasn't sure about putting this story to film, so it was shelved, at least temporarily. There was no other movie project immediately suitable for Ingrid, so she, little Pia, and a Swedish nursemaid stayed in New York, where she would do a six-week run of the Broadway play *Liliom.* Despite her accent, the play won great reviews, as did Ingrid herself.

When the play closed, Petter was able to take leave from the army and come for a visit. Ingrid was eager to show him this exciting city. Unfortunately, where Ingrid saw bright lights, excitement, and tall buildings, Petter only saw dirt and heard obnoxious noises. He was relieved to return to Sweden. While Ingrid's love for New York did not change, her feelings for Petter seemed to take a shift. His obvious dislike of the country she already loved was a terrible disappointment. Still, they decided that living apart wouldn't work.

By the end of 1941, Petter joined Ingrid in Los Angeles on what was hoped to be a permanent basis. It wasn't easy for him to slowly see himself transformed into Mr. Ingrid Bergman and be forced to see an array of handsome men make love to his wife on screen.

Still hopeful that a Joan of Arc movie might still be made, Ingrid made a number of smaller films in 1941, such as *Adam Had Four Sons,Rage in Heaven,* and *Dr. Jekyll and Mr. Hyde.* They were relatively minor productions, but they kept her name and face in front of the movie-going public. Although she could certainly act, her reputation by this point was mostly for her glowing looks.

In 1942, Selznick told Ingrid he wanted her to do a movie called *Casablanca* with Humphrey Bogart. Because there was still a chance to play Joan of Arc, she initially didn't want to join this project. She didn't really think the part of Ilsa had enough to give. In addition, the script kept changing; neither she nor the producers had any idea whether her character would end up with Bogart or Paul Henreid. How was she supposed to prepare for the part if she didn't know who she was going to be with at the end? At first, she assumed the ending was being kept from her to help her acting, but that wasn't the case. No one, whether producer, director, or writer, knew the ending. The making of the movie *Casablanca* could not have been more disorganized.

One day, she met Bogart for lunch. All they had in common was a passionate desire to get out of making this movie. As it happened, Paul Henreid was just as unhappy about doing *Casablanca*. He assumed if he were going to play the secondary role of freedom fighter Victor Laszlo to Bogart's leading character Rick Blaine, he would never become a leading actor. No one seemed to see any potential in what some people now consider the greatest movie ever made. At the time, the people involved in the making of *Casablanca* had no idea what they were creating or that the movie's moral message about sacrificing love for the greater good would have such an immense appeal for the audience.

Renouncing true love was more romantic than any happy ending could have been.

The basic purpose of *Casablanca* was to create a patriotic war movie. When the film begins, a bitter Rick claims, "I stick my neck out for nobody." He has become an indifferent isolationist who cares about no one. One of his staff states, "Rick never drinks with his customers." That fact is, he wants nothing to do with people. His bitterness began years earlier, when his love, Ilsa, deserted him in war-torn Paris. He never knew the reason.

Now, Ilsa comes back into his life as the wife of freedom fighter Victor Laszlo, who is being sought by the Nazis. She begs Rick for help to get them out of Casablanca. Rick is still too hurt to help but, seeing Lazlo's heroism up close, he becomes involved and eventually helps them escape. He is no longer on the sidelines. He has become a patriot and can no longer remain neutral in the war unraveling around him.

Relationships are important in *Casablanca*. Rick and Sam, the black piano player and Rick's partner, have been friends for years. It was extremely rare in the 1940s to see a simple friendship among members of different races. The best black actors could hope for were roles as servants. In *Casablanca*, Rick and Sam are equals.

Rick cannot help but fall in love with Ilsa all over again. Ilsa, a devoted anti-fascist alongside her husband, still loves him and is willing to leave Laszlo for Rick. Rick pretends to agree but knows Ilsa will regret any such decision, and he has too much respect for the freedom fighter to take his wife. The film ends up with Ilsa in love with Rick while leaving Casablanca with Laszlo. No longer feeling neutral, Rick tells Ilsa that fighting the fascists is far more important than their personal feelings.

In perhaps an unintentional humorous twist at the end, Rick ends up convincing Louis Renault, Casablanca's corrupt police official and a former Nazi collaborator, that life does have value. Renault helps Rick get Ilsa and Laszlo on the plane to freedom, after which the two former cynics, now noble characters ready to fight for the resistance, march off into the foggy evening while Rick mutters the famous line, "I think this is going to be the beginning of a wonderful friendship." Undoubtedly, a part of the movie's success was the concept that two indifferent cynics could grow into passionate fighters for good. People could choose their destiny.

Casablanca received good, if not exalted, reviews. It was the seventh-best Hollywood moneymaker of 1943. By 1955, it had earned $6.8 million. Its message still speaks to new generations, and the movie appears frequently on cable television. It is considered one of the greatest movies of all time, a list which includes *Citizen Kane* and *Gone with the Wind*. It won three Academy Awards in 1943 and turned Ingrid Bergman into an important star while elevating Bogart to leading man status.

Chapter Five

Bergman's First Oscar Award

*"The world is a fine place and worth fighting for
and I hate very much to leave it."*

—Ernest Hemingway, *For Whom the Bell Tolls*

Bergman's next role would be in Ernest
Hemingway's *For Whom the Bell Tolls*.
Hemingway rarely became involved with
Hollywood, especially when Tinseltown prepared
to turn one of his novels into a movie. "You
throw them your book, they throw you the
money," he said. "Then you jump into your car
and drive like hell back the way you came."

After selling *For Whom the Bell Tolls* to
Paramount Pictures, however, he was eager to
have them offer the role of Robert Jordan, an
American volunteer fighting in the Spanish Civil
War, to Gary Cooper. Hemingway truly believed
Cooper was perfect for the part, so he fought for

him. As for Ingrid Bergman, he had first noticed her in the American version of *Intermezzo*. While Ingrid looked Nordic, he considered her the ideal actress to play the vulnerable Spanish woman Maria. To truly make his point, he provided her with a copy of *For Whom the Bell Tolls* with the inscription, "You are the Maria in this book."

Since the movie was being made by Paramount, Hemingway first had to persuade Selznick to lend Ingrid out to play the part. Fortunately, Selznick was thrilled at the idea of lending his protégé out for such a high-profile movie, and he personally arranged a systematic publicity campaign for her. He set up a meeting between Bergman and Hemingway and arranged for the lunch meeting to be photographed by *Life* magazine.

But although Selznick went all out for Ingrid, it was to no avail. Paramount gave the part to one of its own contract players, Vera Zorina. In fact, Zorina was already on set and had her hair cut short as the role required when Hemingway stepped in and demanded the part be given to Ingrid instead. Paramount finally relented. They gave Zorina a cash settlement to keep her from suing them for breaking their contract and then called up Ingrid to give her the good news.

For Whom the Bell Tolls became the hit of the year, even greater than *Casablanca* at the time, and Ingrid won an Oscar nomination for her portrayal of Maria. *For Whom the Bell Tolls* was another anti-fascist, anti-war movie. Robert Jordan, played by Cooper, is a volunteer fighting the fascists in the Spanish Civil War. His mission is to destroy a strategic bridge that the fascists need. During this critical mission, Jordan falls in love with Maria, a resistance fighter.

One of the old guerrilla fighters, Anselmo, leads Jordan through the territory. As the guerrillas move toward the bridge, Maria becomes more and more important to Jordan. A lot of Jordan's equipment is destroyed, and he is forced to approach the bridge with nothing but hand grenades. As Jordan sets up the grenades, the guerrilla fighters race for safety. He, however, is hit by a piece of the bridge and is unable to move. Knowing that Maria will die if she remains, he ensures that she leaves the scene. Then, with the help of a Lewis machine gun, he fires at the oncoming fascists without stopping. He will die happy knowing he has saved his beloved Maria.

For Whom the Bell Tolls was a huge success and garnered nine Oscar nominations. It, like

Casablanca, is all about sacrificing for love. It was the second love story in a row where Ingrid did not get her man, but both tales of love lost brought audiences to tears. By the end of shooting for this film, Ingrid's husband Petter, who had been studying medicine at the University of Rochester, received his American medical degree. Now, the entire family was able to settle down in California.

Immediately after, Ingrid and Gary Cooper were paired for another movie, *Saratoga Trunk*. Then, she filmed *Gaslight*, a psychological thriller that introduced the teenaged Angela Lansbury in her first movie role as a scheming, murderous temptress. *Gaslight* was lauded upon its release in 1944 and was nominated for seven Oscars, with Ingrid Bergman winning her first Academy Award for Best Actress. It is the third movie in which the character played by Ingrid makes unfortunate choices about the men in her life. In this movie, she is paired with Charles Boyer, whose devilish plan is to drive her character insane (i.e., gaslight her) while attempting to steal her jewels.

In a flashback, we see a famous opera singer being murdered during the opening scene. The killer flees without getting his hands on her jewelry because he is interrupted by the opera singer's 14-year-old niece, Paula, an orphan raised by the singer. Flash forward many years. Now an adult, Paula, played by Ingrid, marries Gregory Anton, played by Charles Boyer, following a whirlwind courtship. They settle in London in the home of her deceased aunt, locking up her aunt's belonging in the attic to create a new home.

Following the move, strange events keep happening to Paula as she becomes more and more anxious. She misplaces a brooch, although she distinctly recalls putting it in her purse. When a picture disappears, Gregory claims that she took it. Strange sounds are coming from the attic. Gaslights turn off and on by themselves. Gregory tells her she is imagining everything, and Paula starts to worry that she might be losing her mind.

Gregory keeps Paula in the house instead of letting her go out and make friends. He claims this is because of her own fragile mental health. Slowly breaking down, Paula isn't sure what to think and does what her husband tells her. She has no one else in her life. He begins to claim that things around the house are missing, and Paula is the only one who could have taken them. Clearly, she is losing her mind.

Gregory begins to deliberately flirt with a maid (the young Angela Lansbury) and accuses Paula of imagining things. What Paula doesn't know is that the man she married, Gregory, is actually Sergis Bauer, the man who killed her aunt when she was 14 years old. At that time, her presence had prevented him from stealing her aunt's jewels, and he married her to get them. He is the one wandering through the attic searching for the missing gems. Gregory is attempting to drive Paula insane and get a power of attorney putting him in control of her wealth.

Paula has a chance meeting with Brian Cameron, an inspector with Scotland Yard and old admirer of her aunt. Cameron slowly catches on to what Gregory is doing and arrests him. Paula, now understanding the truth, knows she is perfectly sane. She can't resist taunting her husband before he is taken away. "If I were not mad, I could have helped you. Whatever you had done, I could have pitied and protected you. But because I am mad, I hate you. Because I am mad, I have betrayed you. And because I'm mad, I'm rejoicing in my heart, without a shred of pity, without a shred of regret, watching you go with glory in my heart!"

The movie's ending implies that Paula and Cameron will establish a permanent and healthy relationship. Ingrid might finally get a good man—at least in the movies. In real life, her marriage was by this point showing serious strain. Bergman and her family were now settled in a house on Benedict Canyon Drive. Petter was working as an intern, and Ingrid was no longer the blushing 18-year-old he had married. She had turned into a major star, and that could not have been easy for him to take. More and more, he kept criticizing little things she did and how she looked. Cracks were showing in the marriage. It was Ingrid who first broached the subject of divorce, but Petter dismissed it. Being "Mr. Ingrid Bergman" did have some privileges.

Chapter Six

Bergman at the end of World War II

"I've never sought success in order to get fame and money; it's the talent and the passion that count in success."

—Ingrid Bergman

When Selznick wanted to make a movie propagating psychiatry, he chose Alfred Hitchcock as the director. Hitchcock had a reputation for working with beautiful, delicate blondes, such as Grace Kelly and Tippy Hendren, and he wanted Ingrid Bergman as his leading lady to make this film known as *Spellbound*.

The movie takes place in a mental hospital in Vermont. Ingrid, as Dr. Constance Petersen, is the only female doctor and is considered cold and distant by her male co-workers. When the new head of the hospital, Dr. Anthony Edwardes, played by Gregory Peck, arrives, things become complicated. The cool Dr. Petersen seems to melt the moment she lays eyes on the newcomer.

The new Dr. Edwardes does have a few peculiar habits. Strange things seem to set him off until he seems to come to his senses as if nothing had happened. Dr. Petersen investigates and discovers that this Dr. Edwardes has a different signature than the one she has previously seen in one of the doctor's books. She concludes that the newcomer is an imposter, but she is still besotted with him.

When she questions him, he tells her he has amnesia. Although he remembers nothing, he is certain that the real Dr. Edwardes is gone and that he must have killed him. In what must be considered an illogical move even for a suspense movie, Dr. Petersen quits her job at the hospital and runs away with the fake Dr. Edwardes because she is certain he is innocent of any wrongdoing. The audience is uncertain as to just how innocent Edwardes is, which creates the usual Hitchcockian suspense. Is the lovely Ingrid Bergman as Dr. Peterson putting herself in danger? The movie has a famous dream sequence, which was created by artist Salvador Dali. The dream sequence lasts merely two minutes, but it helps the two fleeing doctors to solve the mystery of the real Dr. Edwardes and who killed him.

Ingrid liked working with Hitchcock. She told him honestly that she didn't believe that an intelligent woman, a doctor, would risk her life and job for a mysterious and troubled patient. Hitchcock simply told her, "Fake it, Ingrid. It's only a movie." As convoluted as Hitchcock's plot was, the acting received praise from the critics.

By the time *Spellbound* was released in 1945, the war in Europe was over, but the ruins remained as a horrific reminder of the loss of millions of lives. At this time, Ingrid traveled throughout Europe to entertain the troops. The total destruction of Berlin left her feeling devasted. Many Americans were visiting the concentration camps, but she couldn't bring herself to go. She was half-German. How could she have come from people who committed such evil? The guilt and confusion she felt were overwhelming.

After this visit, she stayed at the Ritz in Paris for a time. There, she met the famous war photographer Robert Capa. He had witnessed the ravages of war for almost ten years and was ready for some diversion. As a sort of joke, he slid a dinner invitation beneath Ingrid's hotel room door. She agreed to meet him. The passion was out of her marriage, and here, she was free of the controls of her studio. She, too, was open to diversion. The two were instantly attracted to each other. They ate in intimate little cafés, walked in the moonlight near the River Seine, and danced the night away in Parisian nightclubs. It was all very romantic and a painful reminder of the true state of Ingrid's marriage.

Ingrid wanted Capa to come to America and had visions of him being a movie photographer in Hollywood. But that was the last thing Capa wanted. He hated being in one place for any length of time. A few years later, he went to photograph the war in Vietnam and stepped on a landmine. He was 40 years old when he died.

Chapter Seven

Saint Bergman

"People saw me in Joan of Arc, and declared me a saint. I'm not. I'm just a woman, another human being."

—Ingrid Bergman

Alfred Hitchcock was still under contract with Selznick when he cast Ingrid in another thriller, *Notorious*, this time opposite Cary Grant and Claude Rains. Grant portrays FBI Agent Devlin, and Ingrid is Alicia Huberman, whose father is a known German spy. Devlin plans on recruiting Alicia for an undercover mission. Alicia is a patriotic American, but her questionable past is used against her, leaving her no choice but to agree to the mission.

Devlin and Alicia have an affair before flying to Rio. In Rio, Alicia is to romance Alexander Sebastian, played by Claude Rains, a Nazi sympathizer whose house is always filled with important scientists with vital information about

Nazi activities. While Devlin hired her for the mission, he is disappointed that she accepted. Maybe she is as notorious as people claim. He doesn't know that Alicia is in love with him.

In Rio, Sebastian, who is also in love with her, wants to marry her. Still upset that she would agree, Devlin tells her to go right ahead. He loves her and is not happy with the situation he himself has created. In effect, he, the spy, is forcing Alicia to sleep with another man. He has no idea that she agrees only because of her love for him.

Alicia marries Sebastian and learns useful secret information from him and his friends, which she provides to Devlin. The only secret she can't unravel is the wine cellar, which is locked. Only Sebastian has the key. Devlin tells him he wants to be invited to a party at Alicia and Sebastian's house, and Alicia is to get him the key to the wine cellar. She does as she is told. During the party, Devlin and Alicia sneak down to the cellar. They discover one of the wine bottles contains lethal uranium, which is used in making atomic bombs.

The two are discovered by Sebastian. Now, Sebastian is facing a dilemma; he can't have Alicia walking around with this secret. His mother suggests that they take care of Alicia by slowly poisoning her. Within days, she becomes sicker and sicker and is unable to make her next appointment with Devlin. He becomes suspicious and sneaks into her room. She tells him she is being poisoned by Sebastian. Sebastian walks in on them. He doesn't want his Nazi friends to discover that he has bungled the bottle with the uranium. Devlin ignores him and carries Alicia to safety. Sebastian is left to his own fate.

Ingrid was a great choice for the role of Alicia. She is both noble while projecting genuine sensuality. Still, Selznick was concerned whether the audience would relate to a woman who is in love with one man and marries another at his instructions. He need not have worried. It was Devlin who placed Alicia in Sebastian's bed and used her as bait. Alicia was merely attempting to please him while Devlin manipulates the scenario and then blames her for her "notorious" behavior. He is perceived as far colder than Ingrid's character.

Notorious was one of the biggest movie hits of 1946 and made its debut in New York City's Radio City Music Hall. In October of that year, Ingrid starred in *Joan of Lorraine* on Broadway, a role for which she won a Tony Award. She was excited to do this as she had admired Joan of Arc all her life. The play is a play-within-a-play depicting a group of present-day actors rehearsing for a drama. Ingrid portrays both the actress playing Joan of Arc and the character of Joan. *Joan of Lorraine* reflects the changes that the play has on the actors staging the play.

Following the run of the play, Ingrid finally got her wish and filmed the movie version of *Joan of Arc*. The film foregoes the play-within-a-play gimmick and is a straightforward portrayal of the life of Saint Joan. Ingrid was nominated for an Oscar for her portrayal but lost to Jane Wyman.

After wrapping up work on this movie, she returned to Petter and Pia in California. She was glad to be home. Still, she had a quiet feeling that something was missing from her life. Her seven-year contract with Selznick was coming to an end in 1947, and she was at a loss of what to do. Many actors were leaving the studio system and working independently. Ingrid just didn't think that was for her.

One day, she and Petter were out for a stroll when they decided to go into a theater playing an Italian film called *Rome, Open City*. Ingrid was eager for some entertainment. As she watched the movie, she was more than entertained and considered the movie a work of genius. She sat through the final credits and noted that the director and writer was one Roberto Rossellini. She was stunned by the brilliance of what she had just seen. All she could think of was, "I have to meet this man." She had no idea how she would go about doing that, but she was unable to forget this movie—or the man who had created it.

Later that year, Ingrid was in New York for a radio show. She wandered past a small, independent artistic theater when she noticed that the move playing—*Paisan*—was directed by the same Roberto Rossellini. She bought a ticket and went to see it. Again, the film stunned her. She kept asking people about Rossellini, but the Italian director was unknown in the country. She wanted to write him a letter of appreciation for his work but had no idea where he lived.

Ingrid got lucky one day when a fellow diner approached her in a restaurant asking for an autograph. The man was Italian. Having nothing to lose, she asked him, "Do you know Roberto Rossellini?" The man smiled. "In Rome, everybody knows Roberto Rossellini." She asked for his address, but the man didn't have that information. What he could tell her was that

Rossellini was associated with Minerva Studios in Rome.

Ingrid sent a fan letter immediately. She wrote, in part, "If you ever need a Swedish actor who speaks very good English and a little German, who can make herself understood in French and can only say 'ti amo' in Italian, then I'll come and make a film with you." When the studio called Rossellini to inform him of the letter, the taciturn director hung up. Ingrid was unaware that Rossellini's relationship with Minerva had ended badly. The studio gave up and simply mailed the letter to his home.

Rossellini later explained that he had no idea who Ingrid Bergman was. He did not know anyone in the Hollywood circle. Then he was reminded of the Swedish version of *Intermezzo*, a movie he had sat through three times. The two hadn't met, but now they were eyeing each other across the pond with considerable interest.

Chapter Eight

Affair with Roberto Rossellini

"A kiss is a lovely trick designed by nature to stop speech when words become superfluous."

—Ingrid Bergman

After making yet another Hitchcock movie, *Under Capricorn,* Ingrid and Petter flew to Paris to meet with Rossellini since Ingrid wanted the iconic director to direct her in a movie. Although everyone present thought this was a great idea, it didn't happen immediately.

A few months later, Rossellini was in New York to accept an award for *Paisan,* the movie that had so impressed Ingrid. Since he was in America anyway, he took the train to Los Angeles to investigate further possibilities. He already had a film, *Stromboli,* in mind for Ingrid. Because he was struggling financially, especially by American standards, a hotel would be expensive, so Petter and Ingrid invited him to stay in their guesthouse.

Petter was mostly busy at the hospital. It was Ingrid, therefore, who showed Rossellini the sights of Los Angeles and accompanied him to the parties to which he was invited. Petter didn't mind. He didn't suspect that Ingrid had any reason to be dissatisfied with their marriage. As far as he was concerned, he was a handsome, successful doctor who had everything to offer a woman. Why would Ingrid look elsewhere?

Ingrid had not yet made a movie for MGM, but Samuel Goldwyn was interested in her. When he contacted her, she agreed to meet him with Rossellini for a possible cooperative venture. Unfortunately, Goldwyn didn't care for Rossellini and the meeting went nowhere. The ever-practical Petter had a suggestion. Howard Hughes was known to finance movies, especially if there was a beautiful woman involved. They contacted Hughes, who agreed to meet with them.

At the meeting, Hughes totally ignored Petter and only addressed Ingrid. He didn't want to hear about any specific movie ideas, nor did he ask how much money was needed. All he asked was whether Ingrid would be dressed and made up beautifully. When the answer was affirmative, he offered her whatever funds she needed. Ingrid was overjoyed. At that moment, no one had any idea just how this meeting would change her life forever.

Ingrid was soon on a plane to Rome. Since she assumed she'd be home in a few weeks, she only took a few items of clothing. Most importantly, she left her daughter Pia behind. She had no idea she wouldn't see her again for many years.

Meanwhile in Italy, Rossellini was ending his relationship with actress Anna Magnani (actually, she ended it by tossing a plate of spaghetti at him in public). He arranged for a huge paparazzi welcome to meet Bergman's flight and set Ingrid up to stay in a suite at the Excelsior Hotel, where he himself kept an apartment.

They didn't start on the movie immediately. Instead, Rossellini drove Ingrid around Italy— Naples, Capri, and other breathtaking sights—as he slowly wowed her. It didn't take much; she was already in love with him. They were in Amalfi when Ingrid wrote Petter a letter. Although she had been vaguely dissatisfied with her marriage and had thought about divorce, she now explicitly spelled out her reasons for a divorce. She apologized but told him that she was absolutely in love with Rossellini. All she could hope for was that Petter would understand.

The two were in the midst of their affair while filming *Stromboli*. In fact, the movie is best remembered for the affair since it made every international headline. In it, Ingrid plays a Lithuanian woman named Karin. Karin is in an internment camp and arranges for her release by marrying an Italian fisherman. The fisherman tells her about his home, Stromboli, and how wonderful everything is where he lives. When they arrive, Karin finds the countryside barren and the simple people of the island unwilling to welcome a foreigner. Eventually, she leaves.

While the movie won an award in Italy, it was panned in the United States. According to the *New York Times*, "After all the unprecedented interest that the picture 'Stromboli' has aroused — it being, of course, the fateful drama which Ingrid Bergman and Roberto Rossellini have made—it comes as a startling anticlimax to discover that this widely heralded film is incredibly feeble, inarticulate, uninspiring and painfully banal." Ingrid herself admitted that if her part had gone to a genuine peasant girl, the movie would have been much better.

Their movie may have bombed, but their affair thrived. It had quickly become major news around the world. Both were still married to other people, and many people in Hollywood claimed to be disappointed in Ingrid. Her behavior was rebuked harshly by the Hollywood Production Code, as well as several churches. She was even denounced by the Senate for moral turpitude, causing Hollywood studios to express reluctance to hire her for anything. It was questionable if she could ever return to America. Petter was unforgiving, and Pia, at the age of 12, understood enough of events to be embarrassed.

In the same month that *Stromboli* was released, Ingrid gave birth to Rossellini's son. They named him Renato Roberto but called him Robin. The press went crazy trying to get pictures. One reporter even checked himself into the hospital where Ingrid was staying. Shortly after Robin's birth, Ingrid and Rossellini obtained their respective divorces and were married. Two years later, in 1952, their twin daughters Isabella and Isotta were born. Pia meanwhile lived with her father and didn't see her mother again until 1957.

Ingrid continued starring in Rossellini's movies. She found that the Italian cinematic world was very different from Hollywood. In Hollywood, things ran as orderly as possible. In Italy, scripts kept changing, and no one ever knew what was going on. It was an adjustment for Ingrid. She had tremendous hopes of being able to stake a claim in the Italian film industry, but it was not to be. The movies she made with Rossellini were lauded as high art, but they simply weren't filling theaters. She didn't achieve the stardom that had been granted her in America.

At this time, she petitioned a California court for permission to have Pia visit her. Petter bitterly opposed that request, stating he didn't want his daughter under the influence of a man like Rossellini. When Ingrid considered flying to California to see her oldest daughter, Rossellini violently objected to her having any contact with Petter. Ingrid was torn between loyalties and didn't know which way to turn.

Although there were a number of talented Italian directors, such as Federico Fellini, Ingrid only made movies with Rossellini. Rossellini would not allow her to appear in anyone else's film. He jealously guarded their relationship without feeling the necessity to be faithful himself. They were an attractive couple and extremely popular in Europe, where their relationship was not censored. It was American tourists that hit them with insults.

Nevertheless, Ingrid's American agent worked diligently on having Hollywood and its audience accept her return to the American cinema. Polls were taken, and Ingrid came out extremely negative. The scandal, especially her leaving behind her young daughter, was too much for some people to accept. Her audience expected her to be pure and perfect; when she acted otherwise, they turned against her.

Refusing to give up, the agent presented Twentieth Century Fox with an excellent script: Ingrid would play the title role in the movie *Anastasia*, with the redoubtable Helen Hayes in the role of the Russian dowager empress. Ingrid jumped at the opportunity to do the film. In *Anastasia*, she plays a disheveled and confused woman who bears an uncanny resemblance to the executed tsar's youngest daughter. She passes every test, including when questioned by the dowager empress. She appears to know things only the real Anastasia could have known. The dowager empress tries to arrange a grand and royal marriage for her. Instead, the woman believed to be Anastasis rejects the offer and marries a commoner. The film leaves vague the answer as to whether she is really Anastasia or not.

The film, which was released in 1956, was well-accepted, and Ingrid was nominated for another Oscar. Still, she didn't feel comfortable returning to America. When she won the Academy Award, it was Cary Grant who went onstage to accept on her behalf.

Meanwhile, now at the age of 18, Pia flew to Europe to see her mother for the first time in years. She tried to fit in with her young half-siblings and stepfather, all the while wondering what Petter would say.

Chapter Nine

Bergman's Third Marriage

"Happiness is good health and a bad memory."

—Ingrid Bergman

Sadly, as Ingrid's grasp of Italian improved, she and Rossellini had less and less to say to each other. It would take more than professional admiration for the relationship to succeed, and they really didn't have that much in common. They were two very different people. And, to make matters worse, their professional collaborations had not been as well-received as they had hoped.

When Rossellini went to India to scout out another movie location, Ingrid heard plenty of rumors of his affair with a married Indian woman named Somali Das Gupta. When she asked him about it, he denied any wrongdoing, but he made repeated frantic phone calls to her (international phone calls were expensive) and asked her not to believe any rumors she might hear. Clearly, he was worried about something.

While Rossellini was making arrangements to return home, his latest mistress, Somali, arrived in Paris a few days ahead of him. The two women met, and Somali admitted to being pregnant with Rossellini's baby. When Ingrid next saw Rossellini, she asked him if he wanted a divorce. Reluctantly, he admitted he did. Both were more relieved than hurt. The marriage that never should have happened was finally over, and what had begun as an international scandal ended with a sad whimper.

Since Italian law forbade divorce, the couple had to apply for an annulment. These were difficult to obtain, but Ingrid's attorney found a technical loophole: it seemed her marriage to Rossellini had been registered before her divorce from Petter by sheer accident. This, technically, made her marriage to Rossellini invalid. However convoluted, a judge finally agreed, and the marriage was legally dissolved.

Peevishly, Rossellini demanded full custody of their three children and took them to a house in Santa Marinella. Ingrid was terrified of losing more of her children. They were Italian citizens, and she was in great danger of not being able to take them to America. In the end, she saw them only on holidays and other special occasions in Rome while they were growing up. Her relationship with Rossellini had cost her a great deal.

Lingering in Paris until the divorce was finalized, Ingrid was playing the lead in the play *Tea and Sympathy*. One night, she was introduced to Swedish producer Lars Schmidt by her agent. Ingrid was depressed over the loss of yet another marriage and more than receptive to Schmidt's overtures. Rossellini was livid when he heard of her new romance. He petitioned the court to have her branded an unfit mother and thus was able to separate Ingrid from three of her children until they turned into adults.

Lars Schmidt had a private island off the coast of Sweden that was his beloved retreat. When he brought Ingrid for a visit, he asked her to marry him. Lars added she should only accept if she loved his island. Ingrid adored the island, and the two were promptly married in 1958. The cabin on the island was rustic and completely without modern amenities; it didn't even have electricity. It was a world away from the fame that Ingrid knew, and she loved it.

Chapter Ten

Return to Hollywood

"She has a combination of rare beauty, freshness, vitality and ability that is as uncommon as a century plant in bloom."

—Film critic about Ingrid Berman

In 1958, Ingrid made a movie for Twentieth Century Fox called *The Inn of the Sixth Happiness*. It was an American film but shot in Wales. After this film was released, Ingrid flew to Los Angeles and attended the Academy Awards as a presenter. She hadn't faced a Hollywood group since her scandalous marriage to Rossellini. Her good friend Cary Grant introduced her. Perhaps to her own surprised, she received a rapturous standing ovation.

Ingrid's legal struggle for her children by Rossellini continued for many years. Meanwhile, she alternated between Hollywood and Europe as she made movies on both continents. Moving between Europe and America made it easier for her to spend time with her children. It did nothing, however, to lessen Rossellini's bitterness and determination that their children should never visit American soil.

Isabella was diagnosed with curvature of the spine, scoliosis, at the age of 13. There were many painful treatments, which the girl endured with Ingrid at her side. At no time, however, would Rossellini relent and allow his daughter to be seen by an American doctor. He was very strict and controlling of both of his daughters. Isabella was 18 years old when she finally left Rossellini's home and came to the United States. Ingrid was beyond delight, as was Pia, who had her younger half-sister move in with her. Soon afterward, Isotta would follow.

In 1969, Ingrid made her first film in Hollywood in many years when she co-starred in *Cactus Flower* with Walter Matthau. Subsequently, she chose to take a small part in *Murder on the Orient Express*, which won her a third Oscar. Ingrid was not afraid to take roles that called for older women.

In 1982, she starred in *A Woman Called Golda*, the story of Israel's prime minister. It was to be Ingrid Bergman's last acting role. Ingrid was a great admirer of Golda Meir, and she admitted to being especially anxious to play the part because she had misjudged the Nazi danger to such an extent during World War II. In addition, her health was slowly deteriorating during the making of the film. She had been diagnosed with breast cancer several years earlier, and it had spread. Ingrid finished the movie by sheer force of will. No one else knew the extent of her struggles.

A few months after *A Woman Named Golda* was released, Ingrid Bergman passed away on her 67th birthday. It was her daughter Pia who accepted her posthumous Emmy Award for her performance as Golda Meir.

Conclusion

The world loved Ingrid Bergman. Her beauty was luminous to the point of being entirely flawless. It was a natural beauty that did not need a lot of makeup, which set her apart from many of the actresses of the 1940s and 1950s.

Ingrid was passionate enough about life to attempt to have it all—marriage, career, and children. In every decision, she followed her heart rather than her logical instincts, often choosing the wrong types of men—specifically, men who mistreated her and were unfaithful. There were even times when she sacrificed her children for love. She invariably regretted these decisions, but she never felt guilty about acknowledging her own needs.

When Ingrid fell in love with Roberto Rossellini, she refused to acknowledge any guilt; she felt what she felt. It cost her much time with her children, whom she fought to see, but she never renounced the affair, despite being denounced as immoral on the U.S. Senate floor.

Although men adored her, Ingrid Bergman was the rare type of woman whom other women also admired. At all times, she was down-to-earth and practical, refusing to wear designer gowns, too much makeup, or even high heels. Her image was that of a genuine person, and that is what people responded to. To many women, even her scandalous affair was an honest acknowledgment of her need to be loved and seen. This was something they could understand.

Ingrid's children adored her, even though she was not the mother-next-door. After her divorce from Petter, Pia hardly saw her for almost eight years. Likewise, when Ingrid divorced Rossellini, she lost custody of her three children by him. Fortunately, she was able to connect with her children when they were adults, and none of them appeared to resent her for her abandonment. Pia indicated she missed her mother terribly, but when Ingrid was around, she was a kind mother and fun person.

What is true is that Ingrid Bergman lived life according to her own standards. She was never perfect and didn't pretend to be; she merely wanted to be happy and loved, something she struggled with most of her life.

Bibliography

Bergman, Ingrid; Burgess, Alan (1980). *Ingrid Bergman: My Story.*

Chandler, Charlotte (2007). *Ingrid: Ingrid Bergman, A Personal Biography.*

Harmetz, Aljean (1992). *Round Up the Usual Suspects: The Making of Casablanca – Bogart, Bergman, and World War II.*

Leamer, Laurence (1986). *As Time Goes By: The Life of Ingrid Bergman.*

Smit, David (2012). *Ingrid Bergman: The Life, Career and Public Image.*

Spoto, Donald (1997). *Notorious: The Life of Ingrid Bergman.*

Printed in Great Britain
by Amazon

86465429R00037